The Satisfied Soul Daily GuideBook

The Satisfied Soul Daily GuideBook

Your Path to Fulfillment

Shoshana Kobrin, MA, LMFT

authorHOUSE®

AuthorHouse™
1663 Liberty Drive
Bloomington, IN 47403
www.authorhouse.com
Phone: 1-800-839-8640

First published by AuthorHouse   09/09/2011

ISBN: 978-1-4670-2542-3 (sc)
ISBN: 978-1-4670-2543-0 (ebk)

Library of Congress Number: 2011916028

Printed in the United States of America

This book is printed on acid-free paper.

CONTENTS

To my beloved grandchild, Lily. May her excitement with life sustain her and fulfill her forever.

Acknowledgments

My heartfelt thanks to those special people who helped bring this project to fruition:

My friends, Angie Logsdon, Idelle Lipman, and Isabelle Johnson for their infinite patience with both my gloomy forebodings and my frenzied excitement during the making of this book.

Ashton Coelho, my office administrator, for her competence and mind-blowing expertise with computer systems.

Kathleen Epperson, editor, who gave me the idea for the book.

Deborah Medvick, editor of the introduction and back cover.

Dawn Harding for her rapid and thorough proof-reading of the manuscript.

Dr. Keith Kaye who showed me my publication path.

And finally, my gratitude to my clients who taught me much of what I know.

"Why follow the steps of another to find out where our dreams will lead us?"

Peter Block

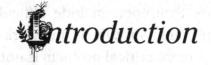# Introduction

"Life is a field of endless possibilities"
Deepak Chopra

Your Path to Fulfillment

The Satisfied Soul Daily GuideBook offers uplifting inspiration and a gentle structure to help you know what's right for you in all areas of life. It's based on my life-long fascination with words and my concept of "soul hunger." Through the years of working with my psychotherapy clients, as well as pursuing my own healing, I learned that no amount of food, money, or sex can satisfy a starving soul. We thrive only when connected to our truest self.

The Power of Words

Since I was a young child, I've been awed by the written word. As soon as I could bike and roller-skate, I'd struggle up the hill to the local library two or three times a week. I was a solitary child. Soon Jane Austen, Dickens, and other authors became my best friends. They opened a window to a world of possibilities beyond my narrow life. Their stories gave me wonder, passion, adventure, and dreams.

As an adult, the power of words was a vital part in healing the wounds from my childhood. I filled notebook after notebook with journal entries and daily goals. Journaling released painful memories while "to-do" lists kept me focused. I've seen this writing practice open vistas of success for both me and my clients.

Soul Hunger

Recovery from bulimia taught me that my *soul* was starving, *not* my body. And that's what I see happening with my clients who have weight and food issues. They are suffering from soul hunger—a deep hunger that cannot be satisfied by feeding the body or losing weight. Connecting with our buried emotions, stifled desires, and latent creativity is the only way to nourish a hungry soul. My clients find that expressing hidden feelings and parts of themselves on paper actually replaces their bingeing, fasting, and purging.

I soon learned that soul hunger also applies to other emotional ills and is a factor in all life's challenges. Symptoms include difficulties in making positive connections with others, the community, living and work situations, and even the everyday world around us. A more critical problem is not being connected to our authentic or Inner Core Self and our Higher Self. Developing nurturing connections and moving with the natural flow of life satisfies a hungry soul.

A Simple, User-Friendly Tool

Journaling can be time consuming and tedious, and you may not want to spend an hour or more a day writing. That's why I made the daily entries of *The Satisfied Soul Daily GuideBook* short, snappy, and to the point requiring little time from your busy schedule. I suggest spending only ten to fifteen minutes to complete an entry. You may find these "snapshot" entries more powerful than longer ones because you focus precisely on what's most important to you. Assessment quizzes allow you to gauge your progress.

The *GuideBook* draws from various spiritual traditions including the mystical Kabala and the teachings of Abraham. These are integrated with models of positive psychology, family systems, attachment theory, and Maslow's theories of self-actualization and motivation.

Over a period of months, I worked with the *GuideBook* myself. In fact, it helped me get out of bed in the morning! I'm amazed at the many surprises in my life since I started completing the daily entries. I found that what I believe, imagine, and think is reflected in my life. Writing down my wishes and desires transformed them into reality. The right people and opportunities entered my life at the right time. I took a new, more fulfilling direction in my spiritual practice. The gentle, nourishing structure of the *GuideBook* helped me to more easily accept the curves that life throws at me. I stay focused on who I am and what I want and need. And most important, my life now feels rich and rewarding!

GuideBook techniques have supported my clients in their steps toward fulfillment. You, too, have the power to transform your life. I hope that you discover new concepts and strategies to take you from scarcity to prosperity and self-actualization. May the everyday miracles and plentiful fruits of our astonishing planet, Earth, nourish your body *and* your soul.

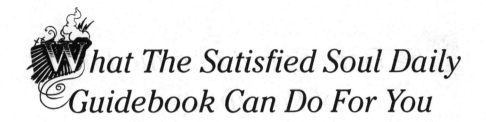

What The Satisfied Soul Daily Guidebook Can Do For You

Perhaps right now you long for a more creative and fulfilled life. Do you wish it were easier, satisfying, with more fun and joy? Are you at the mercy of the "Crazy Monkey Mind"—obsessively thinking, worrying, and planning?

You may already sense there's more to life than climbing out of bed in the morning, brushing your teeth and rushing off to work, school, or your daily activities. Then watching TV and repeating the pattern the next day.

The Satisfied Soul Guidebook offers strategies for changing your thoughts, feelings, and behavior. The aim of the GuideBook is to lead you from anxiety and despondency to the prospect of a new reality. As Greg Anderson said, "When we are motivated by goals that have deep meaning and by dreams that need completion, then we truly live."

The Dark Spiral and the Land of Possibility

I've discovered a secret reason for people's dissatisfaction with life: a negative belief system. Buried deep in their unconscious, far from awareness, is the false belief that they're insignificant and unworthy. They feel their lives have no value. They're convinced no matter how hard they try, they'll never succeed. This is confirmed for them when life refuses them satisfaction and fulfillment.

This negative belief system is a soul hunger, a "Dark Spiral." When we're lost in the inner emptiness of the Dark Spiral, our lives feel mundane, without purpose or hope. So how do we overcome this Dark Spiral?

The answer is in a spiritual approach, the "Land of Possibility," the place of the soul, a space of pure potential. It's very different from the hopeless space of the Dark Spiral. The Land of Possibility is the plowed, fertile field waiting for seeds to be sown, or a vacant piece of land before the house is built. This concept appears in Genesis as the darkness before creation. Your Land of Possibility is indeed fertile and waiting for growth, even if you're not aware of it.

In the Dark Spiral we disconnect from self and life. Are you connected with your desires, dreams, talents, and capabilities? The Land of Possibility offers opportunity for soul satisfaction and vibrant living. As you give yourself permission to discover unknown aspects of yourself, you enter your Land of Possibility. When you develop nurturing connections, you become more accepting of who you are. As Oscar Wilde said, "Be yourself—everyone else is taken!"

Blocks to Satisfying your Soul

Inherited tendencies, biochemical and personality factors, and disruptions during important developmental stages affect soul satisfaction. Our family influences how we feel about ourselves. Many parents, because of their own difficulties in life, fail to engender a healthy sense of self in their children. We bring this absence of the inner self, a soul loss, into the world with us.

Our hungry, consumer-oriented, and addictive culture also contributes to soul loss. Surface values such as wealth, possessions, and looks are paramount. The explosion of technology interferes with intimate, face-to-face relationships. Society conditions us to "do" rather than "be." We are overscheduled and overworked. As T. S. Eliot wrote, "We are distracted from distraction by distraction." And we end up with both our souls and wallets depleted.

Negative patterns of thought, emotion, and behavior we learned as children are unconsciously reinforced and repeated. We hold onto false beliefs that no longer serve us, such as "I'm not supposed to fulfill myself and be happy or confident." I call this the "Hole in the Road." We try to avoid this hole but many of us keep falling back in. We remain empty, unfulfilled, and trapped in the Dark Spiral.

My aim is to help you overcome these challenges by developing what psychologist Carl Rogers termed "unconditional positive regard"—respecting, believing in, and loving yourself. Rather than following the dictates of others and society, learning to tap into your Inner Core Self and Higher Self for guidance.

Assessing your Soul Satisfaction

This assessment evaluates ten important aspects of your life to pinpoint what nourishes you and what you need to change.

1. *Body*
   Are you critical of your body or do you appreciate it? Often we judge ourselves by the shape and weight of our bodies. Do you define yourself by any illness, weakness or pain in your body? To avoid this, some of us also disconnect from positive bodily sensations.

2. *Emotions, Needs, Hopes, and Dreams*
   We tend to numb out difficult emotions which are so hard to bear but this deadens positive feelings as well. Then our needs and wants become grey, dulled, and hard to identify. Are the "musts," "oughts," and "shoulds" that your parents, peers, and the media taught you in conflict with your feelings and true needs? What is missing in your life and what do you long for?

3. *Family*
   Who is your family? If your own family is unsupportive and disconnected from you, your "family" might be close friends, an organization, or a community.

4. *Relationships*
   How satisfactory are your relationships? Assess the different types of relationships in your life—intimate, close, friendly, work-related, and social. Which relationships feel easy to be in? Which are difficult, boring, or tense?

5. *Vocation*
   What are your interests and passions? It's important to feel excitement and enthusiasm about your vocation, whether you are retired, a homemaker, a student, or go to work each day.

6. Living Situation

   How do you feel about where you live? A sense of place, feeling connected to where we live is an important part of satisfying spiritual hunger. Your living situation also includes your financial position. According to Suze Orman, material and spiritual abundance come from the same source.

7. *Community*

   What is your community? In order to feel fulfilled, we need to feel connected to a community and the world beyond ourselves.

8. *Recreation*

   How do you amuse and entertain yourself ? "Recreation" is "re-creation." We recreate ourselves through enjoyable and satisfying pastimes, hobbies, and interests.

9. *Inner Core Self*

   Were you taught to be "nice?" Do you have the courage to be yourself? Or do you hide behind a false self? Pleasing others at the expense of self triggers doubts about who we really are. We wonder whether we're valued beyond our various roles.

10. *Higher Self*

   Are you connected to an inner wisdom or a spiritual power greater than yourself? What gives you a sense of peace and comfort? Perhaps it's a particular place where you worship, meditate, or walk by the sea. When you're distracted by worries and unmet needs, you miss the peace and comfort that prayer, meditation, or a connection with nature offers.

The Satisfied Soul Assessment Quiz

To gauge your progress, take this quiz now. Take it again after thirty and sixty days of completing entries, and when you've accomplished the ninety days of entries. Rate the degree of satisfaction you have with each item on a scale from 1 (poor) to 10 (excellent).

The total of your points reflects the percentage of soul satisfaction you experience.

☐	Body
☐	Emotions
☐	Family
☐	Relationships
☐	Vocation
☐	Living Situation
☐	Community
☐	Recreation
☐	Inner Core Self
☐	Higher Self
☐	Total Score

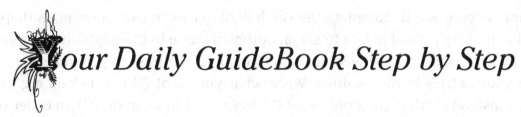Your Daily GuideBook Step by Step

At first glance, your Daily GuideBook may seem simplistic to the point of triteness. But writing is a powerful process. There's a kernel of truth about "I know it's true because I saw it in writing." Your unconscious accepts the written word as truth far more easily than it accepts thoughts or ideas. When you complete a GuideBook page at least five times a week, your mind clarifies and prioritizes your desires and wishes. You need practice, just as you do with learning to play tennis or a guitar. Regular practice with the GuideBook forms an optimistic and compassionate relationship with yourself. Your daily entries will increase your self-awareness, foster mindfulness, and discipline your mind to focus on positive thought.

Journaling with the GuideBook can lead to peace and wholeness. This mini-pause in the morning or after a busy day detaches unwanted emotion, decreases reactivity, quiets your mind, and calms anxiety. It releases you from regrets about the past, feverish plans for the future, and obsessive worries of things to do. As the Buddha said, "We are what we think. All that we are arises with our thoughts. With our thoughts, we make our world."

You might wish, for instance, that you have a creative outlet in your life. Writing day after day "I now have a fascinating hobby" can galvanize you to begin a ceramics class, or take up line dancing. Your GuideBook puts you in touch with the present, the Now, so you notice the scent of the south wind, new buds on the rhododendron, or the comfort of the couch at your back.

This GuideBook is a powerful tool for choosing what nourishes you and avoiding whatever leaves you frustrated and empty. You'll discover which relationships, communities, or job situations work for you and which you're ready to discard. Daily journaling programs your unconscious mind and your Higher Self to either find solutions or to accept with serenity those issues beyond your control.

I've enclosed a sample page of the GuideBook so that you can become familiar with the process. You might want to photocopy the sample page and keep it in front of you until you're used to the method. A page should take you no more than ten or fifteen minutes each day. Use as few or as many of the allotted lines as you wish. Keep your answers simple, brief, and to the point. Don't think too hard—just write down the first thought that comes into your head!

Some people like to complete the GuideBook pages in the morning, perhaps even before they get out of bed to set an optimistic tone to the day. Others prefer the evening, using the GuideBook for preplanning the next day. Remember to frame your entries in the positive. Write what you want ("I am making a good living") instead of what you don't want ("I don't want to be in debt"). In order to achieve your desired results, you need to feel strongly and intensely about your entries.

Your Satisfied Soul Daily GuideBook has ninety days of entries. You can order further sets of entries from my website at www.kobrinkreations.com

Features of Each GuideBook Page

A Asking your Higher Self for help

"Higher Self" is used interchangeably with "God," "The Divine," "Adonai," "Higher Power," "Spirit of Life," or your conception of the force in the universe greater than yourself. The requests to your Higher Self are universal and wide-ranging rather than specific and particular.

B Your wishes for the day

These are particular goals you would like to achieve during the day. They can be as ambitious or trivial as you like. Accomplishing them, or even just writing them down will focus and empower you.

C Your gratitude list

It's so easy to forget we have much to be grateful for. The items you enter can be as big or small as you like. Please remember to include gratitude for who you are and what you have accomplished.

D Imagine you now have exactly what you want

Write down your desires as though they're already in place. As you do this, visualize the positive outcome. i.e. Imagine depositing a large check in the bank, or buying the house you want to live in. Focusing on what you want in life attracts it to you. Negative thoughts do the opposite. What you believe, imagine, and think is reflected in your life. What makes you feel good? With whom you feel comfortable? What gives you pleasure? The Joseph Campbell quote "follow your bliss" is a helpful guide to your needs and wants.

E Ask a question of your Higher Self

Take some deep breaths, relax your shoulders, eyes, and mouth, and go to a quiet place inside yourself to find the right question.

F Write down the response you receive.

Trust whatever answer floats into your mind.

Read your entry, then sign the page. At the end of the day or the next morning, read your entry again. Reflect on any new thoughts that come to mind.

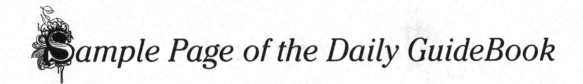

Sample Page of the Daily GuideBook

A To my Higher Self—Please help me to:
Be present and aware
Use my time well and my day profitably
Change my thoughts to the positive

B Today, I want to:
Call up a Susan for a lunch date
Walk and swim
Finish the Janus project at work

C I am grateful:
To Jane, Margaret, and Peter for helping me after my accident
That it's stopped raining and the sun has come out
That I have food enough to eat and a roof over my head

D I already have exactly what I want in life:
I have more than enough money for my needs and am saving every month
My back feels strong and healthy
The right relationship has come my way

E Ask a question of your Higher Self:
What should I do when I feel overwhelmingly anxious?

F Write down the answer you receive:
Breathe, relax your shoulders, mouth and eyes. Remember I'm here to take care of you.

our Daily Entries

DAY 1   Date_____

A | To my Higher Self—Please help me to:

_____
_____
_____

B | Today, I want to:

_____
_____
_____

C | I am grateful:

_____
_____
_____

D | I already have exactly what I want in life:

_____
_____
_____

E | Ask a question of your Higher Self:

_____
_____

F | Write down the answer you receive:

_____
_____

Signed_____

DAY 2   Date_____

A | To my Higher Self—Please help me:
_____
_____
_____

B | Today, I want to:
_____
_____
_____

C | I am grateful:
_____
_____
_____

D | I already have exactly what I want in life:
_____
_____
_____

E | Ask a question of your Higher Self:
_____
_____

F | Write down the answer you receive:
_____
_____

Signed_____

19

DAY 3   Date_____

A | To my Higher Self—Please help me:

_____

_____

_____

B | Today, I want to:

_____

_____

_____

C | I am grateful:

_____

_____

_____

D | I already have exactly what I want in life:

_____

_____

_____

E | Ask a question of your Higher Self:

_____

_____

F | Write down the answer you receive:

_____

_____

Signed_____

DAY 4   Date_____

A │ To my Higher Self—Please help me:
_____
_____
_____

B │ Today, I want to:
_____
_____
_____

C │ I am grateful:
_____
_____
_____

D │ I already have exactly what I want in life:
_____
_____
_____

E │ Ask a question of your Higher Self:
_____
_____

F │ Write down the answer you receive:
_____
_____

Signed_____

DAY 5   Date_____

A   To my Higher Self—Please help me:

_____

_____

_____

B   Today, I want to:

_____

_____

_____

C   I am grateful:

_____

_____

_____

D   I already have exactly what I want in life:

_____

_____

_____

E   Ask a question of your Higher Self:

_____

_____

F   Write down the answer you receive:

_____

_____

Signed_____

DAY 6   Date_____

A | To my Higher Self—Please help me:

_____
_____
_____

B | Today, I want to:

_____
_____
_____

C | I am grateful:

_____
_____
_____

D | I already have exactly what I want in life:

_____
_____
_____

E | Ask a question of your Higher Self:

_____
_____

F | Write down the answer you receive:

_____
_____

Signed_____

DAY 7   Date_____

☐ A ☐ To my Higher Self—Please help me:

_____
_____
_____

☐ B ☐ Today, I want to:

_____
_____
_____

☐ C ☐ I am grateful:

_____
_____
_____

☐ D ☐ I already have exactly what I want in life:

_____
_____
_____

☐ E ☐ Ask a question of your Higher Self:

_____
_____

☐ F ☐ Write down the answer you receive:

_____
_____

Signed_____

DAY 8   Date_____

A | To my Higher Self—Please help me:

_____

_____

_____

B | Today, I want to:

_____

_____

_____

C | I am grateful:

_____

_____

_____

D | I already have exactly what I want in life:

_____

_____

_____

D | Ask a question of your Higher Self:

_____

_____

F | Write down the answer you receive:

_____

_____

Signed_____

DAY 9   Date_____

A│ To my Higher Self—Please help me:

_____

_____

_____

B│ Today, I want to:

_____

_____

_____

C│ I am grateful:

_____

_____

_____

D│ I already have exactly what I want in life:

_____

_____

_____

E│ Ask a question of your Higher Self:

_____

_____

F│ Write down the answer you receive:

_____

_____

Signed_____

DAY 10   Date_____

A │ To my Higher Self—Please help me:
_____
_____
_____

B │ Today, I want to:
_____
_____
_____

C │ I am grateful:
_____
_____
_____

D │ I already have exactly what I want in life:
_____
_____
_____

E │ Ask a question of your Higher Self:
_____
_____

F │ Write down the answer you receive:
_____
_____

Signed_____

DAY 11   Date_____

A │ To my Higher Self—Please help me:

_____
_____
_____

B │ Today, I want to:

_____
_____
_____

C │ I am grateful:

_____
_____
_____

D │ I already have exactly what I want in life:

_____
_____
_____

E │ Ask a question of your Higher Self:

_____
_____

F │ Write down the answer you receive:

_____
_____

Signed_____

DAY 12   Date_____

A | To my Higher Self—Please help me:

_____

_____

_____

B | Today, I want to:

_____

_____

_____

C | I am grateful:

_____

_____

_____

D | I already have exactly what I want in life:

_____

_____

_____

E | Ask a question of your Higher Self:

_____

_____

F | Write down the answer you receive:

_____

_____

Signed_____

DAY 13   Date_____

A | To my Higher Self—Please help me:

_____

_____

_____

B | Today, I want to:

_____

_____

_____

C | I am grateful:

_____

_____

_____

D | I already have exactly what I want in life:

_____

_____

_____

E | Ask a question of your Higher Self:

_____

_____

F | Write down the answer you receive:

_____

_____

Signed_____

DAY 14   Date_____

A | To my Higher Self—Please help me:
_____
_____
_____

B | Today, I want to:
_____
_____
_____

C | I am grateful:
_____
_____
_____

D | I already have exactly what I want in life:
_____
_____
_____

E | Ask a question of your Higher Self:
_____
_____

F | Write down the answer you receive:
_____
_____

Signed_____

DAY 15   Date_____

☐ A To my Higher Self—Please help me:

_____
_____
_____

☐ B Today, I want to:

_____
_____
_____

☐ C I am grateful:

_____
_____
_____

☐ D I already have exactly what I want in life:

_____
_____
_____

☐ E Ask a question of your Higher Self:

_____
_____

☐ F Write down the answer you receive:

_____
_____

Signed_____

DAY 16   Date_____

☐ A To my Higher Self—Please help me:

_____

_____

_____

☐ B Today, I want to:

_____

_____

_____

☐ C I am grateful:

_____

_____

_____

☐ D I already have exactly what I want in life:

_____

_____

_____

☐ E Ask a question of your Higher Self:

_____

_____

☐ F Write down the answer you receive:

_____

_____

Signed_____

DAY 17   Date_____

A | To my Higher Self—Please help me:

_____

_____

_____

B | Today, I want to:

_____

_____

_____

C | I am grateful:

_____

_____

_____

D | I already have exactly what I want in life:

_____

_____

_____

E | Ask a question of your Higher Self:

_____

_____

F | Write down the answer you receive:

_____

_____

Signed_____

DAY 18   Date_____

A | To my Higher Self—Please help me:

_____

_____

_____

B | Today, I want to:

_____

_____

_____

C | I am grateful:

_____

_____

_____

D | I already have exactly what I want in life:

_____

_____

_____

E | Ask a question of your Higher Self:

_____

_____

F | Write down the answer you receive:

_____

_____

Signed_____

DAY 19   Date_____

| A | To my Higher Self—Please help me:

_____

_____

_____

| B | Today, I want to:

_____

_____

_____

| C | I am grateful:

_____

_____

_____

| D | I already have exactly what I want in life:

_____

_____

_____

| E | Ask a question of your Higher Self:

_____

_____

| F | Write down the answer you receive:

_____

_____

Signed_____

DAY 20   Date_____

A | To my Higher Self—Please help me:

_____
_____
_____

B | Today, I want to:

_____
_____
_____

C | I am grateful:

_____
_____
_____

D | I already have exactly what I want in life:

_____
_____
_____

E | Ask a question of your Higher Self:

_____
_____

F | Write down the answer you receive:

_____
_____

Signed_____

DAY 21   Date_____

A | To my Higher Self—Please help me:

_____

_____

_____

B | Today, I want to:

_____

_____

_____

C | I am grateful:

_____

_____

_____

D | I already have exactly what I want in life:

_____

_____

_____

E | Ask a question of your Higher Self:

_____

_____

F | Write down the answer you receive:

_____

_____

Signed_____

DAY 22   Date_____

A | To my Higher Self—Please help me:

_____

_____

_____

B | Today, I want to:

_____

_____

_____

C | I am grateful:

_____

_____

_____

D | I already have exactly what I want in life:

_____

_____

_____

E | Ask a question of your Higher Self:

_____

_____

F | Write down the answer you receive:

_____

_____

Signed_____

DAY 23   Date_____

A To my Higher Self—Please help me:

_____
_____
_____

B Today, I want to:

_____
_____
_____

C I am grateful:

_____
_____
_____

D I already have exactly what I want in life:

_____
_____
_____

E Ask a question of your Higher Self:

_____
_____

F Write down the answer you receive:

_____
_____

Signed_____

DAY 24   Date_____

A To my Higher Self—Please help me:

_____

_____

_____

B Today, I want to:

_____

_____

_____

C I am grateful:

_____

_____

_____

D I already have exactly what I want in life:

_____

_____

_____

E Ask a question of your Higher Self:

_____

_____

F Write down the answer you receive:

_____

_____

Signed_____

DAY 25   Date_____

A | To my Higher Self—Please help me:

_____

_____

_____

B | Today, I want to:

_____

_____

_____

C | I am grateful:

_____

_____

_____

D | I already have exactly what I want in life:

_____

_____

_____

E | Ask a question of your Higher Self:

_____

_____

F | Write down the answer you receive:

_____

_____

Signed_____

DAY 26   Date_____

A | To my Higher Self—Please help me:

_____

_____

_____

B | Today, I want to:

_____

_____

_____

C | I am grateful:

_____

_____

_____

D | I already have exactly what I want in life:

_____

_____

_____

E | Ask a question of your Higher Self:

_____

_____

F | Write down the answer you receive:

_____

_____

Signed_____

DAY 27   Date_____

| A | To my Higher Self—Please help me:

_____

_____

_____

| B | Today, I want to:

_____

_____

_____

| C | I am grateful:

_____

_____

_____

| D | I already have exactly what I want in life:

_____

_____

_____

| E | Ask a question of your Higher Self:

_____

_____

| F | Write down the answer you receive:

_____

_____

Signed_____

DAY 28   Date_____

A │ To my Higher Self—Please help me:

_____

_____

_____

B │ Today, I want to:

_____

_____

_____

C │ I am grateful:

_____

_____

_____

D │ I already have exactly what I want in life:

_____

_____

_____

E │ Ask a question of your Higher Self:

_____

_____

F │ Write down the answer you receive:

_____

_____

Signed_____

DAY 29   Date_____

A To my Higher Self—Please help me:

_____

_____

_____

B Today, I want to:

_____

_____

_____

C I am grateful:

_____

_____

_____

D I already have exactly what I want in life:

_____

_____

_____

E Ask a question of your Higher Self:

_____

_____

F Write down the answer you receive:

_____

_____

Signed_____

DAY 30   Date_____

A | To my Higher Self—Please help me:

_____

_____

B | Today, I want to:

_____

_____

C | I am grateful:

_____

_____

_____

D | I already have exactly what I want in life:

_____

_____

_____

E | Ask a question of your Higher Self:

_____

_____

F | Write down the answer you receive:

_____

_____

Signed_____

Your Satisfied Soul Assessment Quiz #2

To gauge your progress, take this quiz now. Rate the degree of satisfaction you have with each item on a scale from 1 (poor) to 10 (excellent).

The total of your points reflects the percentage of soul-satisfaction you experience.

- Body
- Emotions
- Family
- Relationships
- Vocation
- Living Situation
- Community
- Recreation
- Inner Core Self
- Higher Self

- Total Score

DAY 31   Date_____

A To my Higher Self—Please help me:

_____

_____

_____

B Today, I want to:

_____

_____

_____

C I am grateful:

_____

_____

_____

D I already have exactly what I want in life:

_____

_____

_____

E Ask a question of your Higher Self:

_____

_____

F Write down the answer you receive:

_____

_____

Signed_____

DAY 32   Date_____

A | To my Higher Self—Please help me:

_____
_____
_____

B | Today, I want to:

_____
_____
_____

C | I am grateful:

_____
_____
_____

D | I already have exactly what I want in life:

_____
_____
_____

E | Ask a question of your Higher Self:

_____
_____

F | Write down the answer you receive:

_____
_____

Signed_____

DAY 33   Date_____

A To my Higher Self—Please help me:

_____

_____

_____

B Today, I want to:

_____

_____

_____

C I am grateful:

_____

_____

_____

D I already have exactly what I want in life:

_____

_____

_____

E Ask a question of your Higher Self:

_____

_____

F Write down the answer you receive:

_____

_____

Signed_____

DAY 34 Date_____

A | To my Higher Self—Please help me:

_____
_____
_____

B | Today, I want to:

_____
_____
_____

C | I am grateful:

_____
_____
_____

D | I already have exactly what I want in life:

_____
_____
_____

E | Ask a question of your Higher Self:

_____
_____

F | Write down the answer you receive:

_____
_____

Signed_____

DAY 35   Date_____

A To my Higher Self—Please help me:

_____

_____

_____

B Today, I want to:

_____

_____

_____

C I am grateful:

_____

_____

_____

D I already have exactly what I want in life:

_____

_____

_____

E Ask a question of your Higher Self:

_____

_____

F Write down the answer you receive:

_____

_____

Signed_____

DAY 36   Date_____

| A | To my Higher Self—Please help me:

_____

_____

_____

| B | Today, I want to:

_____

_____

_____

| C | I am grateful:

_____

_____

_____

| D | I already have exactly what I want in life:

_____

_____

_____

| E | Ask a question of your Higher Self:

_____

_____

| F | Write down the answer you receive:

_____

_____

Signed_____

DAY 37   Date_____

A | To my Higher Self—Please help me:
_____
_____
_____

B | Today, I want to:
_____
_____
_____

C | I am grateful:
_____
_____
_____

D | I already have exactly what I want in life:
_____
_____
_____

E | Ask a question of your Higher Self:
_____
_____

F | Write down the answer you receive:
_____
_____

Signed_____

DAY 38   Date_____

A | To my Higher Self—Please help me:

_____

_____

_____

B | Today, I want to:

_____

_____

_____

C | I am grateful:

_____

_____

_____

D | I already have exactly what I want in life:

_____

_____

_____

E | Ask a question of your Higher Self:

_____

_____

F | Write down the answer you receive:

_____

_____

Signed_____

DAY 39 Date_____

A | To my Higher Self—Please help me:

_____

_____

_____

B | Today, I want to:

_____

_____

_____

C | I am grateful:

_____

_____

_____

D | I already have exactly what I want in life:

_____

_____

_____

E | Ask a question of your Higher Self:

_____

_____

F | Write down the answer you receive:

_____

_____

Signed_____

DAY 40   Date_____

A | To my Higher Self—Please help me:
_____
_____
_____

B | Today, I want to:
_____
_____
_____

C | I am grateful:
_____
_____
_____

D | I already have exactly what I want in life:
_____
_____
_____

E | Ask a question of your Higher Self:
_____
_____

F | Write down the answer you receive:
_____
_____

Signed_____

DAY 41   Date_____

A | To my Higher Self—Please help me:

_____

_____

_____

B | Today, I want to:

_____

_____

_____

C | I am grateful:

_____

_____

_____

D | I already have exactly what I want in life:

_____

_____

_____

E | Ask a question of your Higher Self:

_____

_____

F | Write down the answer you receive:

_____

_____

Signed_____

DAY 42   Date_____

| A | To my Higher Self—Please help me:

_____

_____

_____

| B | Today, I want to:

_____

_____

_____

| C | I am grateful:

_____

_____

_____

| D | I already have exactly what I want in life:

_____

_____

_____

| E | Ask a question of your Higher Self:

_____

_____

| F | Write down the answer you receive:

_____

_____

Signed_____

DAY 43   Date_____

A | To my Higher Self—Please help me:
_____
_____
_____

B | Today, I want to:
_____
_____
_____

C | I am grateful:
_____
_____
_____

D | I already have exactly what I want in life:
_____
_____
_____

E | Ask a question of your Higher Self:
_____
_____

F | Write down the answer you receive:
_____
_____

Signed_____

DAY 44   Date_____

A To my Higher Self—Please help me:

_____

_____

_____

B Today, I want to:

_____

_____

_____

C I am grateful:

_____

_____

_____

D I already have exactly what I want in life:

_____

_____

_____

E Ask a question of your Higher Self:

_____

_____

F Write down the answer you receive:

_____

_____

Signed_____

DAY 45   Date_____

A | To my Higher Self—Please help me:

_____

_____

_____

B | Today, I want to:

_____

_____

_____

C | I am grateful:

_____

_____

_____

D | I already have exactly what I want in life:

_____

_____

_____

E | Ask a question of your Higher Self:

_____

_____

F | Write down the answer you receive:

_____

_____

Signed_____

DAY 46   Date_____

A | To my Higher Self—Please help me:

_____
_____
_____

B | Today, I want to:

_____
_____
_____

C | I am grateful:

_____
_____
_____

D | I already have exactly what I want in life:

_____
_____
_____

E | Ask a question of your Higher Self:

_____
_____

F | Write down the answer you receive:

_____
_____

Signed_____

DAY 47   Date_____

A | To my Higher Self—Please help me:

_____

_____

_____

B | Today, I want to:

_____

_____

_____

C | I am grateful:

_____

_____

_____

D | I already have exactly what I want in life:

_____

_____

_____

E | Ask a question of your Higher Self:

_____

_____

F | Write down the answer you receive:

_____

_____

Signed_____

DAY 48   Date_____

A | To my Higher Self—Please help me:

_____

_____

_____

B | Today, I want to:

_____

_____

_____

C | I am grateful:

_____

_____

_____

D | I already have exactly what I want in life:

_____

_____

_____

E | Ask a question of your Higher Self:

_____

_____

F | Write down the answer you receive:

_____

_____

Signed_____

DAY 49   Date_____

A | To my Higher Self—Please help me:
_____
_____
_____

B | Today, I want to:
_____
_____
_____

C | I am grateful:
_____
_____
_____

D | I already have exactly what I want in life:
_____
_____
_____

E | Ask a question of your Higher Self:
_____
_____

F | Write down the answer you receive:
_____
_____

Signed_____

DAY 50   Date_____

A│ To my Higher Self—Please help me:

_____
_____
_____

B│ Today, I want to:

_____
_____
_____

C│ I am grateful:

_____
_____
_____

D│ I already have exactly what I want in life:

_____
_____
_____

E│ Ask a question of your Higher Self:

_____
_____

F│ Write down the answer you receive:

_____
_____

Signed_____

DAY 51   Date_____

A | To my Higher Self—Please help me:

_____
_____
_____

B | Today, I want to:

_____
_____
_____

C | I am grateful:

_____
_____
_____

D | I already have exactly what I want in life:

_____
_____
_____

E | Ask a question of your Higher Self:

_____
_____

F | Write down the answer you receive:

_____
_____

Signed_____

DAY 52   Date_____

A | To my Higher Self—Please help me:

_____

_____

_____

B | Today, I want to:

_____

_____

_____

C | I am grateful:

_____

_____

_____

D | I already have exactly what I want in life:

_____

_____

_____

E | Ask a question of your Higher Self:

_____

_____

F | Write down the answer you receive:

_____

_____

Signed_____

DAY 53   Date_____

A | To my Higher Self—Please help me:
_____
_____
_____

B | Today, I want to:
_____
_____
_____

C | I am grateful:
_____
_____
_____

D | I already have exactly what I want in life:
_____
_____
_____

E | Ask a question of your Higher Self:
_____
_____

F | Write down the answer you receive:
_____
_____

Signed_____

DAY 54   Date_____

A | To my Higher Self—Please help me:

_____

_____

_____

B | Today, I want to:

_____

_____

_____

C | I am grateful:

_____

_____

_____

D | I already have exactly what I want in life:

_____

_____

_____

E | Ask a question of your Higher Self:

_____

_____

F | Write down the answer you receive:

_____

_____

Signed_____

DAY 55   Date_____

A | To my Higher Self—Please help me:
_____
_____
_____

B | Today, I want to:
_____
_____
_____

C | I am grateful:
_____
_____
_____

D | I already have exactly what I want in life:
_____
_____
_____

E | Ask a question of your Higher Self:
_____
_____

F | Write down the answer you receive:
_____
_____

Signed_____

DAY 56   Date_____

A | To my Higher Self—Please help me:

_____
_____
_____

B | Today, I want to:

_____
_____
_____

C | I am grateful:

_____
_____
_____

D | I already have exactly what I want in life:

_____
_____
_____

E | Ask a question of your Higher Self:

_____
_____

F | Write down the answer you receive:

_____
_____

Signed_____

DAY 57   Date_____

A │ To my Higher Self—Please help me:
_____
_____
_____

B │ Today, I want to:
_____
_____
_____

C │ I am grateful:
_____
_____
_____

D │ I already have exactly what I want in life:
_____
_____
_____

E │ Ask a question of your Higher Self:
_____
_____

F │ Write down the answer you receive:
_____
_____

Signed_____

DAY 58   Date_____

A | To my Higher Self—Please help me:

_____

_____

_____

B | Today, I want to:

_____

_____

_____

C | I am grateful:

_____

_____

_____

D | I already have exactly what I want in life:

_____

_____

_____

E | Ask a question of your Higher Self:

_____

_____

F | Write down the answer you receive:

_____

_____

Signed_____

DAY 59   Date_____

A │ To my Higher Self—Please help me:

_____

_____

_____

B │ Today, I want to:

_____

_____

_____

C │ I am grateful:

_____

_____

_____

D │ I already have exactly what I want in life:

_____

_____

_____

E │ Ask a question of your Higher Self:

_____

_____

F │ Write down the answer you receive:

_____

_____

Signed_____

DAY 60   Date_____

| A | To my Higher Self—Please help me:

_____

_____

_____

| B | Today, I want to:

_____

_____

_____

| C | I am grateful:

_____

_____

_____

| D | I already have exactly what I want in life:

_____

_____

_____

| E | Ask a question of your Higher Self:

_____

_____

| F | Write down the answer you receive:

_____

_____

Signed_____

 *Your Satisfied Soul Assessment Quiz #3*

To gauge your progress, take this quiz now. Rate the degree of satisfaction you have with each item on a scale from 1 (poor) to 10 (excellent).

The total of your points reflects the percentage of soul-satisfaction you experience.

- Body
- Emotions
- Family
- Relationships
- Vocation
- Living Situation
- Community
- Recreation
- Inner Core Self
- Higher Self

- Total Score

DAY 61   Date_____

A | To my Higher Self—Please help me:

_____

_____

_____

B | Today, I want to:

_____

_____

_____

C | I am grateful:

_____

_____

_____

D | I already have exactly what I want in life:

_____

_____

_____

E | Ask a question of your Higher Self:

_____

_____

F | Write down the answer you receive:

_____

_____

Signed_____

DAY 62   Date_____

A │ To my Higher Self—Please help me:
_____
_____
_____

B │ Today, I want to:
_____
_____
_____

C │ I am grateful:
_____
_____
_____

D │ I already have exactly what I want in life:
_____
_____
_____

E │ Ask a question of your Higher Self:
_____
_____

F │ Write down the answer you receive:
_____
_____

Signed_____

DAY 63   Date_____

A | To my Higher Self—Please help me:

_____
_____
_____

B | Today, I want to:

_____
_____
_____

C | I am grateful:

_____
_____
_____

D | I already have exactly what I want in life:

_____
_____
_____

E | Ask a question of your Higher Self:

_____
_____

F | Write down the answer you receive:

_____
_____

Signed_____

DAY 64   Date_____

| A | To my Higher Self—Please help me:

_____

_____

_____

| B | Today, I want to:

_____

_____

_____

| C | I am grateful:

_____

_____

_____

| D | I already have exactly what I want in life:

_____

_____

_____

| E | Ask a question of your Higher Self:

_____

_____

| F | Write down the answer you receive:

_____

_____

Signed_____

DAY 65   Date_____

A | To my Higher Self—Please help me:

_____

_____

_____

B | Today, I want to:

_____

_____

_____

C | I am grateful:

_____

_____

_____

D | I already have exactly what I want in life:

_____

_____

_____

E | Ask a question of your Higher Self:

_____

_____

F | Write down the answer you receive:

_____

_____

Signed_____

DAY 66   Date_____

A | To my Higher Self—Please help me:

_____

_____

_____

B | Today, I want to:

_____

_____

_____

C | I am grateful:

_____

_____

_____

D | I already have exactly what I want in life:

_____

_____

_____

E | Ask a question of your Higher Self:

_____

_____

F | Write down the answer you receive:

_____

_____

Signed_____

DAY 67   Date_____

A | To my Higher Self—Please help me:

_____

_____

_____

B | Today, I want to:

_____

_____

_____

C | I am grateful:

_____

_____

_____

D | I already have exactly what I want in life:

_____

_____

_____

E | Ask a question of your Higher Self:

_____

_____

F | Write down the answer you receive:

_____

_____

Signed_____

DAY 68   Date_____

A │ To my Higher Self—Please help me:

_____
_____
_____

B │ Today, I want to:

_____
_____
_____

C │ I am grateful:

_____
_____
_____

D │ I already have exactly what I want in life:

_____
_____
_____

E │ Ask a question of your Higher Self:

_____
_____

F │ Write down the answer you receive:

_____
_____

Signed_____

DAY 69   Date_____

A │ To my Higher Self—Please help me:

_____

_____

_____

B │ Today, I want to:

_____

_____

_____

C │ I am grateful:

_____

_____

_____

D │ I already have exactly what I want in life:

_____

_____

_____

E │ Ask a question of your Higher Self:

_____

_____

F │ Write down the answer you receive:

_____

_____

Signed_____

DAY 70   Date_____

A | To my Higher Self—Please help me:

_____

_____

_____

B | Today, I want to:

_____

_____

_____

C | I am grateful:

_____

_____

_____

D | I already have exactly what I want in life:

_____

_____

_____

E | Ask a question of your Higher Self:

_____

_____

F | Write down the answer you receive:

_____

_____

Signed_____

DAY 71   Date_____

| A | To my Higher Self—Please help me:

_____

_____

_____

| B | Today, I want to:

_____

_____

_____

| C | I am grateful:

_____

_____

_____

| D | I already have exactly what I want in life:

_____

_____

_____

| E | Ask a question of your Higher Self:

_____

_____

| F | Write down the answer you receive:

_____

_____

Signed_____

DAY 72   Date_____

A To my Higher Self—Please help me:
_____
_____
_____

B Today, I want to:
_____
_____
_____

C I am grateful:
_____
_____
_____

D I already have exactly what I want in life:
_____
_____
_____

E Ask a question of your Higher Self:
_____
_____

F Write down the answer you receive:
_____
_____

Signed_____

DAY 73   Date_____

| A | To my Higher Self—Please help me:

_____

_____

_____

| B | Today, I want to:

_____

_____

_____

| C | I am grateful:

_____

_____

_____

| D | I already have exactly what I want in life:

_____

_____

_____

| E | Ask a question of your Higher Self:

_____

_____

| F | Write down the answer you receive:

_____

_____

Signed_____

DAY 74   Date_____

A To my Higher Self—Please help me:

_____

_____

_____

B Today, I want to:

_____

_____

_____

C I am grateful:

_____

_____

_____

D I already have exactly what I want in life:

_____

_____

_____

E Ask a question of your Higher Self:

_____

_____

F Write down the answer you receive:

_____

_____

Signed_____

DAY 75   Date_____

A To my Higher Self—Please help me:

_____

_____

_____

B Today, I want to:

_____

_____

_____

C I am grateful:

_____

_____

_____

D I already have exactly what I want in life:

_____

_____

_____

E Ask a question of your Higher Self:

_____

_____

F Write down the answer you receive:

_____

_____

Signed_____

DAY 76   Date_____

A │ To my Higher Self—Please help me:
_____
_____
_____

B │ Today, I want to:
_____
_____
_____

C │ I am grateful:
_____
_____
_____

D │ I already have exactly what I want in life:
_____
_____
_____

E │ Ask a question of your Higher Self:
_____
_____

F │ Write down the answer you receive:
_____
_____

Signed_____

DAY 77   Date_____

A To my Higher Self—Please help me:

_____

_____

_____

B Today, I want to:

_____

_____

_____

C I am grateful:

_____

_____

_____

D I already have exactly what I want in life:

_____

_____

_____

E Ask a question of your Higher Self:

_____

_____

F Write down the answer you receive:

_____

_____

Signed_____

DAY 78   Date_____

A | To my Higher Self—Please help me:
_____
_____
_____

B | Today, I want to:
_____
_____
_____

C | I am grateful:
_____
_____
_____

D | I already have exactly what I want in life:
_____
_____
_____

E | Ask a question of your Higher Self:
_____
_____

F | Write down the answer you receive:
_____
_____

Signed_____

DAY 79   Date_____

┌───┐
│ A │ To my Higher Self—Please help me:
└───┘
_____

_____

_____

┌───┐
│ B │ Today, I want to:
└───┘
_____

_____

_____

┌───┐
│ C │ I am grateful:
└───┘
_____

_____

_____

┌───┐
│ D │ I already have exactly what I want in life:
└───┘
_____

_____

_____

┌───┐
│ E │ Ask a question of your Higher Self:
└───┘
_____

_____

┌───┐
│ F │ Write down the answer you receive:
└───┘
_____

_____

Signed_____

DAY 80   Date_____

☐A To my Higher Self—Please help me:

_____
_____
_____

☐B Today, I want to:

_____
_____
_____

☐C I am grateful:

_____
_____
_____

☐D I already have exactly what I want in life:

_____
_____
_____

☐E Ask a question of your Higher Self:

_____
_____

☐F Write down the answer you receive:

_____
_____

Signed_____

DAY 81   Date_____

| A | To my Higher Self—Please help me:

_____

_____

_____

| B | Today, I want to:

_____

_____

_____

| C | I am grateful:

_____

_____

_____

| D | I already have exactly what I want in life:

_____

_____

_____

| E | Ask a question of your Higher Self:

_____

_____

| F | Write down the answer you receive:

_____

_____

Signed_____

DAY 82   Date_____

A | To my Higher Self—Please help me:

_____

_____

_____

B | Today, I want to:

_____

_____

_____

C | I am grateful:

_____

_____

_____

D | I already have exactly what I want in life:

_____

_____

_____

E | Ask a question of your Higher Self:

_____

_____

F | Write down the answer you receive:

_____

_____

Signed_____

DAY 83   Date_____

A | To my Higher Self—Please help me:

_____

_____

_____

B | Today, I want to:

_____

_____

_____

C | I am grateful:

_____

_____

_____

D | I already have exactly what I want in life:

_____

_____

_____

E | Ask a question of your Higher Self:

_____

_____

F | Write down the answer you receive:

_____

_____

Signed_____

DAY 84   Date_____

A │ To my Higher Self—Please help me:

_____

_____

_____

B │ Today, I want to:

_____

_____

_____

C │ I am grateful:

_____

_____

_____

D │ I already have exactly what I want in life:

_____

_____

_____

E │ Ask a question of your Higher Self:

_____

_____

F │ Write down the answer you receive:

_____

_____

Signed_____

DAY 85   Date_____

A | To my Higher Self—Please help me:

_____

_____

_____

B | Today, I want to:

_____

_____

_____

C | I am grateful:

_____

_____

_____

D | I already have exactly what I want in life:

_____

_____

_____

E | Ask a question of your Higher Self:

_____

_____

F | Write down the answer you receive:

_____

_____

Signed_____

DAY 86   Date_____

A | To my Higher Self—Please help me:

_____

_____

_____

B | Today, I want to:

_____

_____

_____

C | I am grateful:

_____

_____

_____

D | I already have exactly what I want in life:

_____

_____

_____

E | Ask a question of your Higher Self:

_____

_____

F | Write down the answer you receive:

_____

_____

Signed_____

DAY 87   Date_____

A │ To my Higher Self—Please help me:

_____

_____

_____

B │ Today, I want to:

_____

_____

_____

C │ I am grateful:

_____

_____

_____

D │ I already have exactly what I want in life:

_____

_____

_____

E │ Ask a question of your Higher Self:

_____

_____

F │ Write down the answer you receive:

_____

_____

Signed_____

DAY 88   Date_____

A | To my Higher Self—Please help me:

_____

_____

_____

B | Today, I want to:

_____

_____

_____

C | I am grateful:

_____

_____

_____

D | I already have exactly what I want in life:

_____

_____

_____

E | Ask a question of your Higher Self:

_____

_____

F | Write down the answer you receive:

_____

_____

Signed_____

DAY 89 Date_____

A | To my Higher Self—Please help me:

_____

_____

_____

B | Today, I want to:

_____

_____

_____

C | I am grateful:

_____

_____

_____

D | I already have exactly what I want in life:

_____

_____

_____

E | Ask a question of your Higher Self:

_____

_____

F | Write down the answer you receive:

_____

_____

Signed_____

DAY 90   Date_____

| A | To my Higher Self—Please help me:

_____

_____

| B | Today, I want to:

_____

_____

_____

| C | I am grateful:

_____

_____

_____

| D | I already have exactly what I want in life:

_____

_____

_____

| E | Ask a question of your Higher Self:

_____

_____

| F | Write down the answer you receive:

_____

_____

Signed_____

inal Satisfied Soul Assessment Quiz

Take this quiz now that you have completed your Satisfied Soul GuideBook. Rate the degree of satisfaction you have with each item on a scale from 1 (poor) to 10 (excellent).

The total of your points reflects the percentage of soul-satisfaction you experience.

☐	Body
☐	Emotions
☐	Family
☐	Relationships
☐	Vocation
☐	Living Situation
☐	Community
☐	Recreation
☐	Inner Core Self
☐	Higher Self

☐ Total Score

Epilogue

The root of the Hebrew word *nefesh*, has many branches: breath, respiration, life, refresh, soul, spirit, mind, living being, a person, the self. All these meanings apply to you in your quest for a Satisfied Soul.

The *nefesh*, the soul, is a crystal snared in the primordial mud of being beneath the waves of a thousand oceans all emptying, one into the other, close to the heart of the universe.

Take up your *nefesh*, now, through layers of time and space into the sunlight of a meadow ringed by live oaks. Let her play in the throng of birds and creatures of the wild. Protect her by an arc of rainbows and a circle of light. Let the stars make melody for her by night, and the moon glow on her crystal facets. Each day may she absorb the sun's rays and make them her own.

And beam to you messages from her home in the heavens.

Bibliography

Aftel, Mandy. *The Story of Your Life: Becoming the Author of Your Experience*. New York: Simon & Schuster, 1996.

Aron, Elaine. *The Highly Sensitive Person*. New York: Broadway Books, 1997.

Cameron, Julia. *The Artist's Way: A Spiritual Path to Higher Creativity*. Los Angeles: Jeremy P. Tarcher/Putnam, 1992.

—*The Writing Diet: Write Yourself Right-Size*. New York: Jeremy P. Tarcher/Penguin, 2007.

Davich, Victor. *8 Minute Meditation: Quiet Your Mind, Change Your Life*. New York: Perigee, 2004.

Goldberg, Natalie. *Wild Mind: Living the Writer's Life*. New York: Bantam, 1990.

Hicks, Esther, and Jerry. *Ask and It Is Given: Learning to Manifest Your Desires*. Carlsbad, CA: Hay House, 2004.

Holmes, Jeremy. *John Bowlby and Attachment Theory*. London and New York: Routledge, 1993.

Hopkins, C.J.M. *The Practical Kabbalah Guidebook*. New York: Sterling Publishing, 2001.

Horn, Sam. *Tongue Fu! How to Deflect, Disarm, and Defuse Any Verbal Conflict*. New York: St. Martin's Griffin, 1996.

Johnson, Robert A. *Inner Work: Using Dreams and Active Imagination for Personal Growth*. San Francisco: Harper & Row, 1986.

Kingsolver, Barbara. *Animal Dreams: A Novel*. New York: HarperPerennial, 1991.

Lamott, Anne. *Bird by Bird: Some Instructions on Writing and Life*. New York: Anchor, 1995.

Lang, Diana. *Opening to Meditation: A Gentle, Guided Approach*. Novato, CA: New World Library, 2004.

Maslow, Abraham. *Toward a Psychology of Being*. New York: John Wiley & Sons, 1999.

Munroe, Myles. *Waiting and Dating: a Sensible Guide to a Fulfilling Love Relationship]*. Shippensburg, PA: Destiny Image, 2004.

Newton, Ruth P. *The Attachment Connection: Parenting a Secure & Confident Child Using the Science of Attachment Theory*. Oakland, CA: New Harbinger Publications, 2008.

Orman, Suze. *The Courage to Be Rich: Creating a Life of Material and Spiritual Abundance*. New York: Riverhead, 1999.

Page, Susan. *If I'm so Wonderful, Why Am I Still Single? Ten Strategies That Will Change Your Love Life Forever*. New York: Viking, 1988.

Ross, Ruth. *Prospering Woman: A Complete Guide to Achieving the Full, Abundant Life*. Mill Valley, CA: Whatever Pub., 1982.

Roth, Geneen. *Women Food and God*. New York: Simon & Schuster, 2011.

Seligman, Martin. *Authentic Happiness: Using the New Positive Psychology to Realize Your Potential for Lasting Fulfillment*. New York: Free Press, 2002.

Tillich, Paul. *The Courage to Be*. New Haven, CT: Yale UP, 1952.

Tolle, Eckhart. *The Power of Now: a Guide to Spiritual Enlightenment*. Novato, CA: New World Library, 1999.

Yerkovich, Milan, and Kay. *How We Love: a Revolutionary Approach to Deeper Connections in Marriage*. Colorado Springs, CO: WaterBrook, 2006.

About the Author

Shoshana was born in Johannesburg, South Africa, and started her professional life as a preschool teacher. After taking a Master's degree in literature, she pioneered a multi-cultural communications program during apartheid in South Africa. Her manual, *Communicate While You Teach* was written for teachers and nurses in training.

Interest in intercultural group dynamics led her to a Masters degree in psychology at John F. Kennedy University, Orinda, California, when she arrived in the United States. She is a licensed Marriage Family Therapist, practicing in Walnut Creek, California. Specializations are: people in transition, couple counseling, child therapy, food and weight issues, hypnotherapy, and EMDR. Shoshana teaches at university level, supervises interns, and provides continuing education for therapists and nurses.

For thirty-two years, Shoshana has been teaching, training, public speaking, and facilitating workshops and retreats in the community. She has presented at twelve, state-wide, professional conferences. Publications include poetry, a short story, and articles on food and weight issues, eating disorders, addictions, relationships, spirituality, communication, the family, and parenting. Her self-help book, *The Satisfied Soul: Transforming Your Struggles with Food and Weight* will be published early in 2012.

Books, reading, and writing have been an important part of Shoshana's life since childhood. Two tools were invaluable in healing from a difficult childhood and many years of bulimia: Natalie Goldberg's, *Wild Mind*, which introduced her to free, associative journaling, and Buddhism's *Vipassana* meditation technique. Her spiritual and creative life, which she defines as "connection in many spheres of life" is of prime importance to her.

Shoshana lives in Walnut Creek. She enjoys swimming, hiking, singing, playing the piano and guitar, sketching, and ceramic sculpture.

You are invited to visit my web site for the following information:

- Ordering more copies of this book or extra journal entry pages
- Ordering copies of *The Satisfied Soul: Transforming Your Struggles with Food and Weight*
- Upcoming Retreats and Workshops
- Individual, couple, or child therapy
- A retreat or workshop at your place of worship, school, or community organization. A list of workshops and retreats is available.

www.kobrinkreations.com